STAMP IT!

LARK
KID'S
CRAFTS

STAMP IT!

50 AMAZING PROJECTS TO MAKE

Joe Rhatigan & Rain Newcomb

LARK BOOKS
A Division of Sterling Publishing Co., Inc.
New York

Series Editor: Joe Rhatigan
Art Director: Kathleen Holmes
Photographer: Evan Bracken
Cover Designer: Barbara Zaretsky
Illustrator: Orrin Lundgren
Production Assistance: Shannon Yokeley
Editorial Assistance: Delores Gosnell
Proofreader: Jeanée Ledoux

Library of Congress Cataloging-in-Publication Data
Rhatigan, Joe.
    Stamp it! : 50 amazing projects to make / by Joe Rhatigan, Rain Newcomb.— 1st ed.
      p.   cm. — (Kids' crafts)
    Includes index.
    Summary: Provides step-by-step instructions for using stamps to decorate clothing, party
        decorations, gifts, and much more, as well as for making one's own stamps.
    ISBN 1-57990-504-8
    1. Rubber stamp printing.   [1. Rubber stamp printing. 2. Handicraft.]
    I. Newcomb, Rain. II. Title. III. Series.
TT867.R43 2004
761—dc21   2003010177

10 9 8 7 6 5 4 3 2 1

First Edition

Published by Lark Books, a division of
Sterling Publishing Co., Inc.
387 Park Avenue South, New York, N.Y. 10016

© 2004, Lark Books

Distributed in Canada by Sterling Publishing,
c/o Canadian Manda Group, One Atlantic Ave., Suite 105
Toronto, Ontario, Canada M6K 3E7

Distributed in the U.K. by Guild of Master Craftsman Publications Ltd., Castle Place,
166 High Street, Lewes, East Sussex, England BN7 1XU Tel: (+ 44) 1273 477374,
Fax: (+ 44) 1273 478606, Email: pubs@thegmcgroup.com, Web: www.gmcpublications.com

Distributed in Australia by Capricorn Link (Australia) Pty Ltd.,
P.O. Box 704, Windsor, NSW 2756 Australia

If you have questions or comments about this book, please contact:

Lark Books
67 Broadway
Asheville, NC 28801
(828) 253-0467

Manufactured in China

1-57990-504-8

Contents

Stamping Madness in One Easy Lesson

True or False?
Circle the correct answer.

T   F   With a little piece of rubber or foam and some paint you can transform a boring pair of sneakers into something glamorous and cool.

T   F   Little old you can take some leaves and other stuff from nature and turn a plain canvas bag into an awesome fashion statement.

T   F   All that's standing between you and a fabulously decorated book cover is a piece of bubble wrap, some paint, and a paper bag.

If you answered "True" to all the above questions, **congratulations**, this book is for you. You realize that the wonderfully mad world of stamping is a limitless opportunity to create fun, beautiful, stunning, funny, and engrossing projects, gifts, and decorations.

If you answered "False" to all the above questions, **congratulations**, this book is for you. You are about to realize that the wonderfully mad world of stamping is a limitless opportunity to…Well, you get what we mean.

Whether you know about stamping or not, this book is chock full of project ideas, techniques, information, and more for kids who want to decorate, create, and play around with stamps. The great thing about stamping is that you don't need to know much to get started. You also don't need to buy much. Questions?

What Is Stamping, Anyway?

Stamping is taking a rubber, foam, homemade, or found object, applying some ink or paint to it, and printing the image, shape, or design onto cards, socks, dog bowls, jackets, picture frames, and just about anything else you can think of.

What Do I Need to Get Started?

A couple of stamps, something to stamp on, some ink, and this book.

Is Stamping Addictive?

Highly.

What's in the Book?

Fifty creative projects with step-by-step instructions, a bunch of ways for you to make your own stamps, and everything you need to know to get started.

When Can I Get Started?

Right away. So, what are you waiting for? Class dismissed. Turn the page!

Getting Started

Whether you're brand new to stamping or you consider yourself an old pro, read this chapter before jumping into the projects. We'll fill you in on what you need and how to stamp.

The Stamps

Once you start stamping, you may never stop. It's fun buying rubber or foam stamps, and it's even more fun making your own. Here is just a sampling of the stamps you can use for the projects in this book.

Store-Bought Stamps

You can buy rubber or foam stamps in all shapes and sizes, though foam stamps tend to be less intricate in their design.

Rubber stamps are the most popular type of store-bought stamp. They're easy to use and, with proper care, will last a long time.

Foam stamps usually have bold designs on them.

Homemade Stamps

Sometimes the one stamp you're looking for just doesn't exist. Luckily, making your own stamps is easy. You can make stamps out of cardboard, string, meat trays, erasers, and more. Instructions for several versions appear throughout this book.

A small selection of homemade stamps that appear throughout this book.

The Three Most Important Things to Remember When Making Your Own Stamps

1 When you're carving a stamp, the areas that stick up will be the colored-in areas.

2 Go slow. You can always carve more material off, but you can't put it back on.

3 Your stamp will be the reverse of the image you carve. If you want to stamp a word or number, !DRAWKCAB TI ETIRW

You can make stamps out of fruit. Potato carving is an old favorite. See page 28.

9

Found Stamps

Sponges, potato mashers, bubble wrap, body parts, and more can be used as stamps. It won't be long before you're finding lots of fun things you never thought could be used as stamps.

If it's got a neat outline, texture, or if it's just plain cool, stamp it! Clockwise from left: shoe, computer parts, mesh, shelf liner, bubble wrap, and more mesh.

Sponges are great for stamping backgrounds.

What other objects can you find in nature to use as stamps?

Inks and Paints

What kind of ink or paint you use to stamp with depends on what you're stamping on.

✔ Dye-based inks are thin, water-based inks that are available in pads or markers. (The markers are called printing pens or brush markers.) Use these inks with detailed stamps. These inks dry quickly, although they tend to bleed on paper and fade over time.

✔ Also available in pads or markers, pigment inks are thicker and are made so that they won't bleed with other colors on paper. It takes a longer time for these inks to dry, and they won't dry at all on glossy paper. Pigment inks tend not to fade.

✔ You can use acrylic paints to stamp on wood and other materials.

✔ Crafter's ink is good for wood, fabric, shrink plastic, and metal.

You can get any kind of ink in a pad made especially for stamping.

Fabric paints can be used for stamping on fabric. Read the instructions on the containers before using. You can also find fabric ink pads and markers in craft stores.

Printing pens work just like markers.

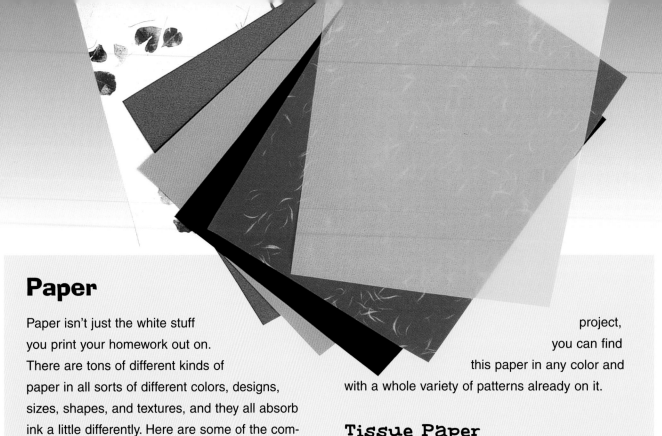

Paper

Paper isn't just the white stuff you print your homework out on. There are tons of different kinds of paper in all sorts of different colors, designs, sizes, shapes, and textures, and they all absorb ink a little differently. Here are some of the common types of paper:

Card Stock

This is the most versatile paper. It's smooth and has a fairly heavy weight, which means it's thicker and stiffer than the pages of this book. It comes in all sorts of colors and patterns, and you can get it in a matte (not shiny) or glossy finish (very shiny). If you use pigment inks on glossy card stock, you'll have to heat-emboss the stamped image in order to set the ink (see page 45). The ink won't sink into the paper otherwise.

Text Weight

This paper is a lot like computer paper. If you don't want to decorate the background of your project, you can find this paper in any color and with a whole variety of patterns already on it.

Tissue Paper

Tissue paper is fun to stamp on. It's very fragile, so you'll have to be gentle with it. Dye-based inks work best on tissue paper.

Vellum

This smooth, see-through paper comes in text weight and card stock. It's glossy, so you're better off using dye-based inks or using the heat-embossing technique on page 45.

12

Other Materials and Tools

You've got your stamps. You've got your inks and paints. Now what? Here are the rest of the tools and materials you need to get yourself going.

You never know when you're going to want to draw a temporary line on your project to keep everything lined up. Keep a pencil and ruler on hand so that you're ready to make that line anytime. A ruler is handy for when you want to stamp in grids or patterns. Draw guiding lines onto your project lightly in pencil. After you've stamped everything (and let the ink dry) go back and erase the lines. And, of course, you can't live without scissors.

Also, cover your work surface with newspaper. Not only will it keep the table clean, but you'll also be able to test your stamps on it. You should also stamp on top of a stack of scrap paper or newspaper. The paper creates a very nice padding to press the stamps into as you print them. (This makes your stamped images show up better.) Use paper towels for cleaning up your stamps. Wet ink is a lot easier to clean up than dry ink, so keep those paper towels within reach.

A brayer is a hand-held roller that you can use to ink stamps or create backgrounds.

Inking the Stamp

Depending on what kind of ink you're using, you'll use different methods to get the ink onto the stamp.

Using Ink Pads

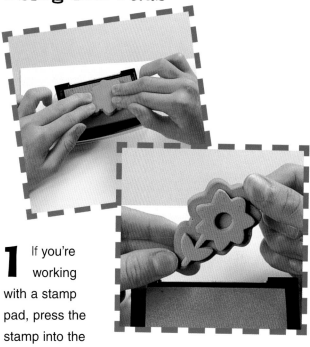

1 If you're working with a stamp pad, press the stamp into the pad gently. You have to be careful not to get too much ink on your stamp, so just set the stamp on the ink pad and tap the back of it gently. (Sometimes it works better to press the pad to the stamp.)

2 Test the stamp on a piece of newspaper to see how well you inked the image. You can usually stamp several times before re-inking.

13

Using Pens

1 If you're using the printing pens to ink your stamps, simply place your stamp right side up in front of you and start coloring.

2 Apply the lighter colored markers first and work your way to the darkest. That way you won't contaminate your colors.

Using a Foam Paintbrush

1 Pour some of the paint onto wax paper or a paper plate.

2 Dab the brush in the paint and brush it onto the stamp. This technique may require some practice as you figure out just how much (or how little) paint you need. Do lots of test stamps on newspaper.

Using a Brayer

1 Pour some ink onto a smooth, flat surface, such as a piece of wax paper or a paper plate.

2 Roll the brayer back and forth over the ink or paint until it gets tacky.

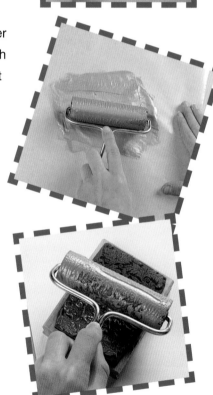

3 Roll the brayer across the surface of the stamp.

Coloring Stamps

Coloring stamps with printing pens is a great way to add flair to your images. It works really well on foam stamps that don't have too much detail. If you use these techniques on highly detailed stamps, remember that you need to color in only the raised areas.

Coloring Stamps with Different Sections

A lot of foam stamps have different sections already separated and ready to color in. To work with these stamps, simply use the printing pens to color in the different sections of the stamp.

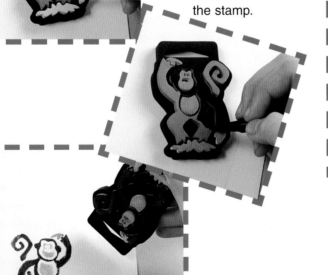

Rainbow Stamps

To give your image a rainbow look when you stamp it, select several different colors of printing pens. Put them in the order you want to use them and start coloring at one edge of the stamp with the lightest color. Then color another section with a darker color. Make sure to work from lightest to darkest so that the colors don't mix and get muddy. Don't worry if the edges are mixing where the colors meet. This will add to the rainbow effect. When you're finished coloring, stamp.

15

Making Patterns on Stamps

You can also use printing pens to make a pattern on your stamp. Decide what kind of pattern you want. Then, start to color the stamp with the lightest color marker you'll use. Work your way up to the darkest color.

Special Tip

If it takes you a really long time to color in your stamp, breathe on it before stamping it. This will remoisten any ink that might have dried.

Stamping on Paper, Fabric, Wood, or Whatever

You'll get better at this step the more you do it, so don't freak out if you don't do it perfectly the first time.

Four Easy Steps to Success

1 If you're stamping on paper, set the paper on several pieces of scrap paper or newspaper. Ink the stamp.

2 Gently set the inked stamp on your paper. Be careful not to wiggle it or move it around at all after you've set it down. The image will blur if you do.

3 Press the back of the stamp evenly with your hands or fingertips. Make sure you get the center and all of the edges.

4 Carefully lift the stamp straight up and off the paper. Set it aside and look at the stamped image.

Troubleshooting

✔ If the whole image on the stamp didn't print, try it again. Make sure the stamp is fully inked. You may want to put it on a different part of the ink pad just in case part of the pad has gone dry.

✔ When you stamp the image, make sure that you're applying the same amount of pressure over the whole stamp.

✔ If the image didn't print clearly or the details of the stamp were blurry, you might have too much ink on your stamp. Clean off the ink with a paper towel and try it again. Be gentler when you press the stamp into the ink pad, or try using the brayer to ink the stamp. If you're still having trouble, try it with thinner ink.

✔ If the image is blurry and smeared, you probably got a little too jumpy when you were placing it on the paper. Be very careful not to bump, shake, or wiggle at all when you're stamping the image. Don't rock it back and forth either. One of the best ways to get a blurry image is to put your stamp where you think you want it and then decide that it should actually be just a little bit to the right (or the left, or wherever). Don't try even the teeniest adjustment on the stamp after it has made contact with the paper. Instead, use the pencil and the ruler to make light placement guides *before* you start stamping.

More Thoughts on Stamping

➥ When stamping on wood, follow the instructions for stamping on paper, but make sure to use pigment ink pads or acrylic paints.

➥ When stamping on fabric, put a piece of cardboard on your work surface or inside a shirt, sock, or pillowcase before stamping. This will keep any ink or paint from seeping through the front side and onto the back. Also, make sure you're using fabric ink, and have an adult help you set the dye so you can wash the project.

➥ When stamping on metal, use metal paint.

17

Fun Ways to Decorate Your Stamped Images

Just because you stamped a bunch of images on a project doesn't mean you have to be finished.

Chalks

Colored chalks have a light look sort of like watercolors. They're not always easy to control in small, tight areas.

First, stamp the image with a dark ink and let it dry. Then make small circles of color with the chalk. Use your fingers to smear the color around. Don't forget to wash your fingers off before using another color. If you're using more than one color, make sure to start with the lighter colors and work your way to the darker colors. After you've colored in your stamp completely, spray the image with a matte-finish sealer to keep the chalk from rubbing off.

Colored Pencils

Colored pencils are great for coloring in stamps.

First, stamp the image with a dark ink and let it dry. Then, color it in with the colored pencils. Cross-hatching is a fun technique for this. Color in one direction and then work in the opposite direction. If you feel like having a little color adventure, use a different color when you scribble in the opposite direction. Sharp points work best for filling in small areas, and dull points are great for covering larger areas with a softer shade of color. You can also use crayons, of course.

Markers

You can use regular markers or printing pens to color in your stamped images. This technique gives you the boldest, brightest colors.

First, stamp the image with a dark ink and let it dry. Then color it in with the markers. If your markers have two different ends, a skinny one and fat one, use the skinny end to color in the details and the small areas and the fat end to color in the bigger areas. Work from your lightest color to your darkest to avoid having the colors mix together and get muddy looking. Be careful not to go over the same spot too many times. The color will get really dark and you'll be able to see the brush marks. The color might also run if you put too much on.

Watercolor Paints

Watercolor paints will give your stamps a soft, artistic look. And because you're being artistic, don't be too concerned about staying in the lines!

First, stamp the image with a dark ink and let it dry. Wet the paintbrush and make tiny circles with it in the first color you want to use. Test the color on a piece of scrap paper to see if it's too light or too dark. If it's too dark, add more water. If it's too light, dab some of the water out of the paint with a clean paper towel and try it again. When you've got the color you want, start painting. Use a thin brush for painting in the smaller areas.

Restamping

Sometimes one stamp just isn't enough. You can do some really interesting things by stamping over the same stamp with a different color. Stamp your first image, clean off the stamp, and wait for the ink to dry completely. Then re-ink the stamp with a different color and place it over the first stamp. Don't worry too much about getting the stamp lined up in exactly the same place as before—not only is it impossible, but it also won't look nearly as cool.

Cleaning Up

What!? Stamping is supposed to be fun, and cleaning up doesn't sound like fun. Well, maybe it's not, but cleaning up your stamps and workspace immediately after you finish a project will make it a lot more fun to return to your stamping later.

Cleaning Your Stamps

As tempting as it might be to submerge your inky stamps in a sink full of sudsy water, don't. The water will make the glue that holds the stamp to the handle come apart. If you immediately wipe off your stamps with a damp paper towel, you shouldn't have too much trouble keeping them squeaky clean. If you do run into trouble, use an old toothbrush to scrub the ink off the stamp's surface. If that doesn't work, dilute window cleaner with some water and use that to clean up the ink. Permanent inks have to be removed with a special cleaning solution.

Putting It All Away

After you've washed every speck of ink (more or less) off your stamps, dry them with an old towel. Gather all of your ink pads and markers. Make sure ink pad lids and printing pen caps are tightly closed.

Put all of your stamps, inks, papers, scissors, and other supplies in a big cardboard box. Store your papers flat, ink pads upside down, and stamps clean, dry, and image-side down.

Now you have a portable studio. Decorate the box with, of course, stamped designs! Now, when inspiration hits, all you have to do is pull out the box and start stamping.

The Projects

Now, without further delay, without a single solitary word to the wise, with no more fooling around, here they are: the wonderful, fantastic projects...plus, a few final words.

You can choose from 50 projects here, including several ways to make your own stamps. Start small and easy and work your way up to the projects that may seem challenging. Also, you can do these projects exactly as they appear in the book (you can even purchase the same stamps used in the projects; see page 110) or branch out on your own. Take a project and run with it. Work with the stamps you like or have. Let your imagination go wild. It's up to you how you approach these projects, as long as you get an adult to help you when necessary. With some practice and patience you'll find that even if you thought your dog had more artistic talent than you did, your projects will look pretty cool. See if your dog can top that. All that really matters is that you enjoy yourself. Okay, we mean it now. No more words. We're done. Now it's your turn.

Dive on in!

Starlight Gift Wrap

You can create a card or a gift tag with the same stamp you use on the gift wrap.

→ Snowflake star stamp

→ White ink pad

→ Tissue paper

→ Pencil with unused eraser

WHAT YOU DO

1 Choose the color tissue paper that you want to use. Lay the paper flat on your work surface. Put a scrap piece of tissue paper behind it since the stamp ink may go through the first layer and onto the table you're working on.

2 Stamp the star randomly over the paper with white ink, rotating the stamp as you go to add some variety.

3 Ink the pencil eraser. (It's now a stamp!) Use it to fill in between the stars.

4 Let the ink dry before using the wrapping paper. When wrapping the present, add another sheet of plain unstamped tissue paper behind the stamped paper. The tissue paper is see-through, and adding another sheet will make it easier to see the stamps and not get a peek at what's inside.

Giant Duffel Bag

This bag is great for sleepovers and vacations
(plus, it'll hold all the dirty clothes from your bedroom floor).

WHAT YOU NEED

→ Flower-shaped cookie cutter

→ Flower-shaped eraser

→ Assorted foam stamps

→ Fabric paint ink pads in assorted colors

→ 1 yard of fabric or large pillowcase

→ Matching thread

→ Sewing machine

→ Iron and ironing board

→ 2 yards of ribbon, 1 inch wide

→ Scissors

→ Large safety pin

→ Cardboard

→ Paper towel

WHAT YOU DO

1 If you don't want to do any major sewing, simply use a big pillowcase, cut a hole in the "tunnel" around the opening of the pillowcase, and skip to step 6.

2 Wash and dry the fabric. If you don't know how to sew, get an adult to help you. Fold the fabric, right sides together, and sew down the long seam and across one of the shorter seams.

Leave the other side open. You now have what looks like a big pillowcase, inside out.

3 Have an adult help you press the seams open with the iron. Press down the top raw edge 2 inches to create a hem. Press the raw edge of opening under ½ inch. Then fold it over again, making a 2-inch overlap.

4 Sew the hem in place, leaving a 6-inch opening in the seam to thread the ribbon through.

5 Stitch a buttonhole on the outside of the bag in the hem, or simply cut a ½-inch-wide opening to stick the ribbon ends through.

6 Pin the safety pin to one end of the ribbon. Thread it all the way around the inside of the hem or tunnel. Pull both ends of the ribbon through the buttonhole or cut in the hem. Stitch the ends of the ribbon together.

7 Sew the 6-inch opening shut. Be careful not to sew into the ribbon. Turn the duffel bag right side out and iron it.

8 Cut a piece of cardboard and place it inside the duffel bag. Stamp the front side of the bag and let it dry.

9 Stamp the other side of the bag and let it dry.

10 Put a paper towel over the stamped areas and have an adult help you iron over it to set the paint. Another way to set the fabric is to throw it in the dryer on medium heat for 30 minutes.

Sunny Citrus Picture Frame

Leave a good impression with this cool stamping technique.

WHAT YOU NEED

→ Orange

→ 2 lemons

→ Lime green, orange, lemon yellow, and tangerine acrylic paints

→ Paintbrush

→ Wooden picture frame

→ Kitchen cutting board

→ Kitchen knife*

→ Paring knife*

→ Spoon

→ Paper towels

→ Wax paper

→ Foam paintbrush

→ Scrap paper

→ Fine-tip paintbrush

*Ask an adult to help you cut and prepare the fruit.

WHAT YOU DO

1 Paint the frame with the lime green paint. Let it dry.

2 Place the orange on top of the kitchen cutting board. Use the kitchen knife to cut the orange in half, horizontally slicing through the middle of the fruit.

5 While the orange dries, repeat steps 2 through 4 with two lemons.

3 Use the paring knife to cut the flesh out of one half of the orange, while leaving the raised divisions intact. Carefully scoop out the fruit with the spoon.

4 Once the flesh is removed from all sections, drain the remaining juice from the orange half onto a paper towel. Repeat with the other half, then allow the orange halves to air-dry for about 30 minutes.

6 Pour some orange acrylic paint onto the wax paper. Use the foam paintbrush to paint the orange, then stamp it onto a piece of scrap paper. If your stamp is too heavy, press the fruit

on the paper again without applying additional paint. Use the fine-tip paintbrush to fill in any orange skin sections that aren't taking paint. Repeat this testing process until you're happy with the results.

7 Stamp the orange onto your frame. Vary the placement of the orange stamps on your frame, and even let a few trail off the edges. Let the paint dry.

8 Repeat using the yellow paint and one lemon half. Repeat again with the second lemon half and the tangerine paint.

Fruits and Veggies

EVEN IF YOU DON'T LIKE THE WAY MUSHROOMS TASTE, YOU MIGHT LIKE THE WAY THEY LOOK—ESPECIALLY AFTER YOU TURN THEM INTO STAMPS. MAKING STAMPS OUT OF FRUITS AND VEGETABLES IS A GREAT WAY TO CREATE UNIQUE DESIGNS.

Mushroom Stamps

1 Cut a mushroom in half and dab the flat side with a paper towel. This will get rid of any excess moisture and give you a clean, dry surface to ink.

2 Ink the mushroom with an ink pad, foam paintbrush, or brayer and stamp it.

3 Don't eat the inked mushroom!

Other Fruits and Veggies

You can use this technique with just about any fruit or vegetable. Try stamping with a pear or apple. You probably can't stamp with a tomato or any other really, really wet fruit or veggie because the ink won't stick to it. If you work up an appetite while stamping, remember to eat ink-free fruits and veggies—not your stamping supplies.

The Famous Potato Stamp

Perhaps the most famous of all vegetable stamps is the potato stamp.

1 Make sure you have adult supervision when making a potato stamp. To make your first potato stamp, start out using a cookie cutter that will fit inside the potato as a guide.

2 Slice the potato in half lengthwise and press the cookie cutter into it.

3 Slice around the cookie cutter with a kitchen knife and remove all the flesh outside the image.

4 Make sure the image that you'll be stamping sticks up at least $1/4$ inch so that the ink will go only on the image and not the background.

5 Ink the potato and stamp it.

6 When you're ready to create your own designs in the potato, slice it in half and draw your design onto it with a felt-tipped marker.

7 Then carve away the excess potato. (Remember, carve away the part that you don't want to be inked.)

Hand Towel

Hands down, this is the most awesome towel ever.

WHAT YOU NEED

→ A hand (or two)

→ Assorted colors of non-toxic fabric paints

→ Terry cloth or fine-weave cotton hand towel, prewashed and dried

→ Cardboard

→ Wax paper

→ Foam paintbrush

→ Small paintbrush (optional)

→ Paper towels

→ Iron or use of a clothes dryer

30

WHAT YOU DO

1 Lay the towel flat on top of a piece of cardboard.

2 Place some paint onto the wax paper. If you're using a brightly colored towel, be sure to use bright paints in contrasting colors that will show up well. Use the foam paintbrush to paint onto the surface of one hand.

3 Press that hand firmly onto the surface of the towel. (Practice on some newspaper first.)

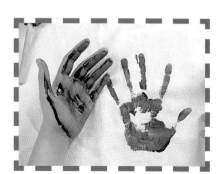

4 Slowly lift your hand off of the towel as you would a stamp.

5 Do it again. If you're switching to another color, wash the hand before repeating. Vary the direction of the handprint for an energized, fun look. Repeat the direction of the print in order to create a graphic pattern.

6 If more definition is needed on some of the prints, use the paintbrush to add paint where needed.

7 Either place some paper towels over the dry handprints and have an adult help you iron over them, or place the towel in the dryer on medium heat for 30 minutes.

31

Simply Divine Sneakers

These shoes have the best of both worlds: they're comfortable AND glamorous.

WHAT YOU NEED

→ Shoe stamp
→ Fabric ink pad and pen in colors of your choice
→ Canvas tennis shoes
→ Newspaper

WHAT YOU DO

1 Stuff the shoes with newspaper and remove the shoelaces. Make sure the paper is in there snugly so the sneaker is firm enough to stamp on.

2 Ink the shoe stamp. Make sure you get plenty of ink on it.

3 Stamp the shoe. Stamp it again. And again. And again. Do this for as long as you want. Color in some of the stamped images with fabric ink pens if you want.

Dog Bowl and Mat

Hey, even dogs deserve to dine in style.

WHAT YOU NEED

→ Knife, fork, spoon, dog, bone, and fire hydrant stamps

→ Red metal paint

→ Red, black, and silver fabric paint

→ Scissors

→ Piece of heavy canvas or foam

→ Foam paintbrush

→ Metal dog bowl

→ Silver glitter fabric paint

→ Paintbrush

→ Acrylic spray sealer

WHAT YOU DO

1 Cut a bone shape out of the canvas or foam. Set it aside.

2 Apply the red metal paint to the bone stamp with the foam brush and stamp it around the edge of the dog bowl. Let it dry.

3 Put the dog bowl in the center of the canvas and stamp the knife, fork, and spoon around it. Stamp the dog, bone, and fire hydrant on the canvas. Use the silver glitter fabric paint to accent the fork, knife, and spoon images.

4 Once the mat is dry, spray it with the sealer.

Hypnotic CD Clock

You're getting sleepy. At the count of three you'll fall into a deep, deep sleep. When you wake up, you won't remember making this cool clock.

WHAT YOU NEED

→ Homemade or purchased spiral stamp (see page 38)

→ Numbers stamps

→ Star stamp

→ Red and black ink pad

→ Paintbrush

→ Gold and black acrylic paint

→ Wooden clock face*

→ Old CD

→ Glue

→ Clock template on page 108

→ Pencil

→ Black and red acrylic paint

→ Paintbrush handle with round end

→ Clockworks and clock hands*

*Available in the clock-making section of the craft store

WHAT YOU DO

1 Paint the wooden clock face as shown in the photo, or forget the photo and strike off on your own.

2 Ink the spiral stamp and print it onto the CD. Let it dry. If you use pigment ink instead of paint, it will take about a day to dry.

3 Glue the CD to the center of the wood circle.

4 Enlarge the clock template on page 109 to fit your clock to help you position your numbers. Place the

photocopy over the clock and mark the number positions with a pencil. Stamp the numbers onto the clock face.

5 Stamp stars between the numbers.

6 Dip the handle of the paintbrush in the red paint. Use it to stamp dots around the clock face in between the stars.

7 Once all the ink has dried, attach the clockworks and hands to the clock according to the clockworks instructions.

Cardboard Stamps

The project on the previous page used a homemade cardboard stamp. Here's how to make it. For a different look, simply change the width of the spiral you draw. Or use string to create a spiral on the cardboard.

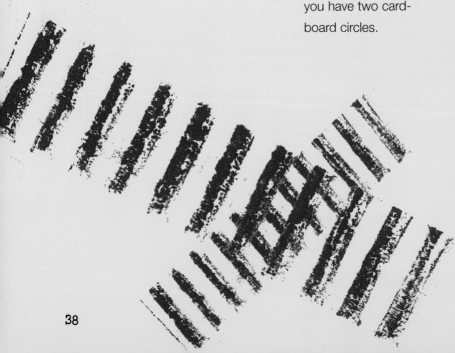

WHAT YOU NEED

→ CD

→ 2 pieces of cardboard

→ Pen

→ Scissors

→ Glue

WHAT YOU DO

1 Place the CD on top of one of the pieces of cardboard. Trace around the CD with the pen and cut it out. Do it again so that you have two cardboard circles.

2 Draw a spiral on one of the cardboard circles.

38

More Cardboard Fun

HEY DUDE, CARDBOARD'S COOL. REALLY, IT IS. ESPECIALLY CORRUGATED CARDBOARD—IT MAKES A GREAT STAMP. THE TEXTURE LOOKS GREAT IN THE BACKGROUNDS OF YOUR PROJECTS.

TO MAKE A CORRUGATED CARDBOARD STAMP, SIMPLY CUT THE CARDBOARD TO THE SHAPE YOU WANT. THEN PEEL THE PAPER OFF OF ONE SIDE SO THAT THE CORRUGATED PART INSIDE THE CARDBOARD IS EXPOSED. INK IT WITH A STAMP PAD, FOAM PAINTBRUSH, OR BRAYER, AND STAMP TO YOUR HEART'S CONTENT!

3 Cut it out and glue it to the other cardboard circle.

Too Cool Bandannas

Fashionable, fun, and easy to make!

Your-Name-Here Scarf

WHAT YOU NEED

→ Name stamp

→ Black fabric paint

→ Bandanna

→ Plastic jewels

→ Small paintbrush

→ Glue

WHAT YOU DO

1 Place a piece of cardboard on your work surface, and place the bandanna face up on top of it.

2 Stamp your name onto the bandanna with the black fabric paint. Let it dry.

3 Put a paper towel over the stamped areas of the bandanna and have an adult help you iron over it to set the paint. Another way to set the fabric is to throw it in the dryer on medium heat for 30 minutes.

4 After the paint has been set, decorate the bandanna with the plastic jewels. Brush glue onto the back of each jewel and press it into place.

40

Lip Scarf

WHAT YOU NEED TO MAKE A NAME STAMP

→ Your favorite stamp-making technique

→ Scrap paper

→ Tracing paper

→ Pencil

WHAT YOU DO

1 Pick your favorite stamp-making technique.

2 Write your name in cool letters on a piece of scrap paper. Trace over the letters with the tracing paper and pencil.

3 Flip the tracing paper upside down on the stamp-making material and rub the back of it to transfer your design.

WHAT YOU NEED

→ Lip stamp

→ Red and pink fabric paint

→ Scrap cardboard

→ Pink bandanna

→ Paper towel

→ Iron or use of a clothes dryer

→ Small paintbrush

→ Red glitter glue

WHAT YOU DO

1 Follow the instructions for the previous scarf, but use the lip stamp and the red and pink fabric paint.

2 After the paint has been set, use the small paintbrush to highlight the lips with the red glitter glue.

Flower Power Cards

Here are just three examples of the thousands of beautiful and professional-looking cards you can create with stamps.

Orange Card

heat-emboss the stamped image (see page 45) if you want.

WHAT YOU NEED

→ Flower, letter, and grass stamps

→ Purple and green printing pens

→ White, green, and red ink pads

→ Orange card and envelope

→ Clear embossing powder and heat gun (optional)

→ Craft knife (get an adult's help)

WHAT YOU DO

1 Unfold the card and lay it flat in front of you. Color in the flower stamp with the purple and green printing pens. Stamp it so the top of the flower is above the fold line.

2 With an adult's supervision, heat-emboss the stamped image (see page 45) if you want.

Green Card

3 Ink the letter stamps with the white ink and stamp the name of the person the card is for below the flower. Heat-emboss the letters.

4 Ink the grass stamp with the green ink pad, stamp it along the bottom of the card, and emboss the images.

5 Ink the small flower stamp with the red ink pad and stamp it randomly across the background of the card.

6 With the craft knife, carefully cut around the part of the main flower stamp that is above the folded line. Refold the card so that the top of the flower sticks up.

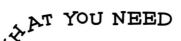

WHAT YOU NEED

→ Flower stamp

→ Black ink pad

→ Green card and envelope

→ Copper embossing powder and heat gun (optional)

→ Scissors

WHAT YOU DO

1 Ink the flower stamp and stamp it once along the bottom edge of the card.

2 With an adult's supervision, heat-emboss the stamped image if you want (see page 45 to learn how to heat-emboss).

3 Stamp and emboss more flowers the way you just did. Remember to stamp one on the flap of the envelope.

4 Use the scissors to cut away some of the paper around the bottom edge of the flowers. Follow the lines of the embossed images.

Flower Power Cards

Yellow Card

WHAT YOU NEED

→ Flower and grass stamps

→ Purple and green printing pens

→ White card stock

→ Clear embossing powder and heat gun (optional)

→ Scissors

→ Yellow card and envelope

→ Craft knife (get an adult's help)

→ Glue

WHAT YOU DO

1 Ink the flower stamp with the purple printing pen. Stamp it onto the white card stock once.

2 With an adult's supervision, heat-emboss the image (see page 45) if you want.

3 Repeat steps 1 and 2 until you have stamped and embossed six flowers. Cut out all of the flowers.

4 Arrange five of the flowers on the front of the yellow card. Trace around three of them with the green printing pen. Unfold the card and cut out the area inside of the green line with the craft knife.

5 Position three flowers inside of the card so that they'll show through the windows you just cut out. Make the windows bigger if you need to, then run the green printing pen along the edge. Glue the flowers into place on the inside and outside of the card.

6 Glue the last flower to the outside of the envelope. Ink the grass stamp with the green printing pen and stamp it along the borders.

Heat Embossing

With this technique, you can create raised and shiny stamped images. It's simple and fun, and the results look fabulous. You need to use a heat gun to emboss, so make sure you have an adult's supervision.

WHAT YOU NEED

→ Stamps

→ Ink pad

→ Whatever you want to stamp on

→ Embossing powder and heat gun*

→ Scrap paper

*Available in the stamping section of craft stores

WHAT YOU DO

1 Ink the stamp and stamp it onto your project.

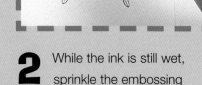

2 While the ink is still wet, sprinkle the embossing powder over it.

3 Tap the excess embossing powder off the project. You can put it back in its container and reuse it later. If you tap the powder onto a piece of scrap paper, you can fold the paper in half and use it as a funnel to pour the extra powder back into the container.

4 Preheat the heat gun for about 10 seconds. Have an adult hold it 4 inches above the project to melt the embossing powder. You'll see the powder melt, rise up, and get shiny. This shouldn't take longer than 15 seconds or so.

5 Once the powder is melted and smooth, turn off the heat gun. Let the stamp cool completely before touching it.

Big Birthday Platter

You don't have to have your own ceramics kiln for this project.
Simply check around town for the nearest ceramics studio.

AT YOU NEED

→ Foam birthday stamps

→ Ceramic paints*

→ Platter*

→ Pencil

→ Small paintbrushes in various sizes

*The paint-your-own ceramics studio will provide these items.

WHAT YOU DO

1 Ceramics studios that provide unglazed ceramics for you to decorate can be found easily in most areas. Look in the telephone directory under "greenware" or "ceramics" to locate one. Though ceramic studios often have their own stamps you can use, bring your own in case they don't have exactly what you want.

2 It's a good idea to plan your design as much as possible before going to the studio. When you've chosen the piece you want to stamp, use a pencil to mark where you'll place

the stamps. The pencil marks will disappear in the kiln.

3 Apply the paint to the candle stamp with a paintbrush. Carefully stamp it on the platter. Brush more paint on the candle stamp and stamp it as many times as you like.

4 After the paint has dried (it shouldn't take too long), accent the candles by painting on a different color applied with a small brush.

5 Brush the paint on the party hat stamp and stamp it around the rim. After the paint

dries, accent the hats with different colors. You can also accent the hats with a glaze that stands out like puffy paint.

6 Simply leave the platter with the ceramics studio and pick it up when they've fired it.

Sunflower Lampshade

This lampshade will add a little sunshine
(or at least some artificial light) to your life.

WHAT YOU DO

1 Paint the dark yellow paint onto the petals and the center of the sunflower stamp. Brush one side of each petal with the bright yellow paint and the other side with the orange paint.

2 The tricky part of this project is how to stamp onto the lampshade. Your best bet is to put one hand on the inside of the lampshade to support it, and then stamp the sunflower onto the shade where your hand is located. Make sure you have plenty of paint on the stamp to get a good image. If you need to, touch up the stamped image with the paintbrush.

WHAT YOU NEED

→ Sunflower stamp

→ Dark yellow, bright yellow, and orange fabric paint

→ Small paintbrush

→ Fabric lampshade

→ Hot glue gun and glue sticks

→ Approximately 50 small silk sunflowers

→ Craft glue

→ Sunflower seeds

3 Stamp the flower around the entire shade. Let the paint dry.

4 Hot glue the silk sunflowers to the top and the bottom edge of the lampshade. (Be careful not to touch the tip of the glue gun or the hot glue itself.)

5 Use the craft glue to attach sunflower seeds to the center of each stamped sunflower.

Paper Bag Book Cover

What's so great about a brown paper bag?
Well, use some found stamps and find out.

WHAT YOU NEED

→ Bubble wrap, shelf liner with a cool texture, and any mesh-like material to use as stamps

→ Assorted colors of acrylic paint

→ Scissors

→ Brown paper bag

→ Book to cover

→ Pencil and ruler

→ Small piece of paper

→ Tape

→ Wax paper

→ Foam paintbrush

→ Brayer

WHAT YOU DO

1 Cut open the paper bag and place it, print side up, on your work surface. Open the book you're going to cover and put it on top of the paper bag.

2 Cut the paper bag 3 inches around the book on all sides.

3 Fold the bag along the top and bottom edges of the book. Crease the edges.

4 Center the book on the bag and fold the edges of the bag over the cover. Set the book aside.

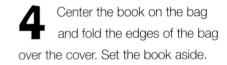

50

5 Flip the book cover over so the nonprinted side is facing you. If you want to write your name on the cover, tape a small piece of paper onto the front of the book cover where you'd like your name to go.

6 Cut the bubble wrap and the shelf liner to be the length of the book cover. Cut a 2-inch square out of the mesh for the hooked rug.

7 Put the different colors of paint onto the wax paper.

8 Use the foam brush to ink the bubble wrap with whatever color paint you want. Place the stamp on the paperbag and roll over it with the brayer. Repeat with the shelf liner and mesh.

9 After the cover has dried, remove the piece of paper you taped on in step 5. Write your name or the name of your book in there. Cover your book.

The Monkey

To make this book cover, get a monkey stamp, a yellow printing pen, and a brown printing pen. Color the face, belly, and hands of the monkey yellow. Color the rest of the monkey brown and stamp it.

Garden Party

You can make all of the accessories for this party or just a few.
Hey, it's your party.

WHAT YOU NEED

→ Bug stamps

→ Alphabet stamp set

→ White and black stamp pads

→ Pencil with unused eraser

→ Scissors

→ 1/16-inch hole punch

→ Glue

→ Stapler

Invitations

WHAT ELSE YOU NEED

→ Green card stock

→ Plain white greeting cards with envelopes

WHAT YOU DO

1 Cut pieces of the green card stock so each piece is 1/2 inch smaller all around than the plain white greeting cards.

2 Using the white stamp pad, stamp a bug on each of the pieces of green paper. Use the pencil eraser to color in the stamp. It should be a little bigger than the stamp itself. Let it dry.

3 With the black stamp pad, stamp the same bug on top of the colored-in stamp. Use the alphabet stamps to stamp your message on the bottom of the invitations.

4 Use the 1/16-inch hole punch to punch a curved flying trail behind the bug (see project photo).

5 Glue the green paper on top of the white cards.

A BIRTHDAY PARTY

Garden Party

Centerpiece

WHAT ELSE YOU NEED

→ Yellow, pink, and green card stock

→ Straws

→ Vase

→ River rocks or sand

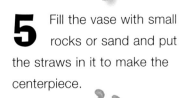

WHAT YOU DO

1 Cut twelve 2 x 4-inch rectangles from the colored card stock.

2 Fold the pieces of paper in half, unfold them, and lay them flat on the table.

3 Using the same technique you used for stamping the invitations, stamp a bug on each piece of paper. Create the flying trails with the hole punch.

4 Fold the paper over the tops of the straws, and staple them.

5 Fill the vase with small rocks or sand and put the straws in it to make the centerpiece.

Straws

WHAT ELSE YOU NEED

→ Yellow and pink card stock

→ Green straws

WHAT YOU DO

1 Cut a ½ x 4½-inch piece of yellow or pink paper for each straw.

2 Fold each piece of paper in half to crease it. Unfold it and lay it flat on your worktable.

3 Using the same technique you used for stamping the invitations, stamp a bug on the right-hand side of each piece of paper.

4 Wrap the paper around the straw and staple it together right next to the straw.

5 Use the 1/16-inch hole punch to punch a flying trail behind the bug.

Napkins

WHAT ELSE YOU NEED

→ Pink paper napkins

WHAT YOU DO

1 Stamp a bug in white in the top right corner of each napkin.

2 Use the 1/16-inch hole punch to create the flying trail behind the insect.

Plates

WHAT ELSE YOU NEED

→ 1/8-inch hole punch

→ Green paper plates

→ Hemp string

→ Yellow card stock

WHAT YOU DO

1 With the 1/8-inch hole punch, punch an even number of holes around the edge of each plate.

2 Cut a 4-foot length of hemp for each plate.

3 Cut a 2-inch-square piece of yellow card stock to make a name tag for each plate. Using the same technique you used for stamping the invitations, stamp a bug on each piece of paper.

4 Using the alphabet stamps, stamp the name of each person attending the party onto the name tag.

5 Use the 1/16-inch hole punch to punch a flying trail behind the bug. Punch a hole in the top left corner with the 1/8-inch hole punch.

6 Thread the hemp string through the holes in the plate. Put a name tag square on the string. Tie the ends together under the rim of the plate and trim the leftover string.

Party Hats

WHAT ELSE YOU NEED

→ Pink card stock

WHAT YOU DO

1 Cut 2-inch-wide strips of paper lengthwise from the card stock. Staple together the narrow ends of two of them for each party guest.

2 Stamp bugs along the strips of paper, about 4 inches apart. Use the same method used for the invitations. Don't forget the flying trails.

3 Form a circle with the strips of paper, and staple the ends together.

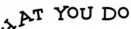

TAYLOR

Garden Party

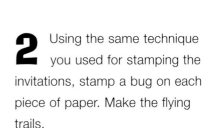

Garland

WHAT ELSE YOU NEED

→ Pink, yellow, and green card stock

→ Hemp string

WHAT YOU DO

1 Cut a length of the hemp string 8 inches longer than the length of the garland you want.

2 Cut the paper into 2½ x 4½-inch pieces. Make three for every foot of garland you're making.

3 Fold pieces of paper in half, unfold them, and lay them flat on the table. Using the same technique you used for stamping the invitations, stamp a bug on each piece of paper. Make flying trails for the bugs.

4 Fold the paper over the garland, alternating the colors and spacing them evenly along the garland. Staple the paper close to the string twice along the top and once on the bottom.

Gift Bags

WHAT ELSE YOU NEED

→ Yellow card stock

→ Brown paper lunch bags

→ Assorted party favors

→ ⅛-inch hole punch

→ Hemp string

WHAT YOU DO

1 Cut a piece of 2½ x 3¼-inch yellow paper for each guest.

2 Using the same technique you used for stamping the invitations, stamp a bug on each piece of paper. Make the flying trails.

3 Fill each bag with the party favors. Fold the top of the lunch bag over twice.

4 Place the yellow paper on the front of the bag. With the ⅛-inch hole punch, create two holes through the yellow paper and the front of the paper bag.

5 Cut a 7-inch length of hemp string. Put the paper in place and thread the string through the holes. Tie it off inside the bag and trim the ends.

56

Polymer Clay Notepad Cover

Here's a great way to add some interest to an otherwise ho-hum notepad.

Polymer Clay Notepad Cover

WHAT YOU NEED

- Alphabet and number rubber stamps
- Interesting computer connectors or other found stamps
- Ink pads in fun colors
- Pliers
- Small spiral notepad
- Rubber band
- 2 ounces of yellow polymer clay
- Plastic rolling pin (don't use a wooden one) or acrylic rod
- Piece of paper
- Plastic coffee stirring straw or toothpick
- Butter knife or polymer clay cutting blade
- Baking tray
- Use of an oven
- Heavy book

WHAT YOU DO

1 Use the pliers to gently straighten out the bent wire end on one side of the notepad's spiral. Unwind the wire spiral from the notepad and set it aside. Remove the front cover and put a rubber band around the rest of the notepad to hold it all in place. Set that aside, too.

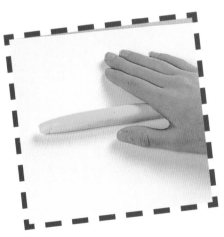

2 Squeeze and knead the clay until you can roll it into a snake. Fold the snake a few times, roll it out, and fold again. Continue rolling and folding until it's soft and warm. (This is called conditioning the clay, and if you don't condition it, your finished project may break.)

3 Flatten the clay with the palm of your hand. Then use the plastic rolling pin or rod to roll the clay into an 1/8-inch-thick sheet. Lay the sheet onto a piece of paper.

4 Place the notepad cover on top of the clay sheet. Use the butter knife or cutting blade to trim away the

58

excess clay around the notepad cover. Trim the clay exactly along the edge with the holes, but make it a little larger on each of the other three edges.

 Use the coffee stirring straw to cut out the holes for the spiral.

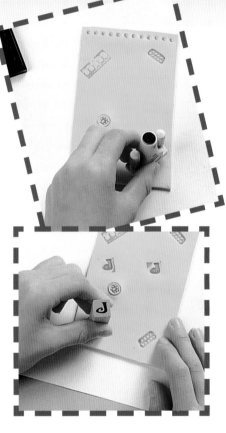

 Remove the notepad cover and leave the clay on the paper. Ink the stamps and computer connectors to make interesting designs on the piece of clay. Be careful not to push the stamp all the way through the clay. Let the ink dry for a few minutes.

7 Put the clay (on the paper) onto the baking tray and bake according to the clay manufacturer's instructions.

 When it has finished baking, remove the clay from the oven and weigh it down with the heavy book. When it's completely cool, line up the clay cover with the rest of the notepad and wind the wire spiral back into place. Bend the end of the wire with the pliers to hold the wire in place.

Note: Wash your hands thoroughly after using polymer clay, and don't use kitchen utensils that will be used for food again.

Doorway Curtain

Buy a big bag of paper key tags at an office supply store, and stamp away!

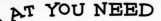
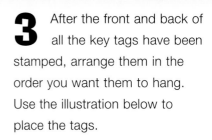

WHAT YOU NEED

→ Small homemade (see page 62) or purchased stamps in random designs

→ Ink pads in various colors

→ 150 paper key tags, 1¼ inches in diameter*

→ Templates on page 109 (optional)

→ ⅛-inch hole punch

→ String or hanging rod

*Available at most office supply stores

WHAT YOU DO

1 Lay out the key tags on your work surface. Set 18 of them aside.

2 If making your own stamps, use the templates on page 109 if you want. Stamp the key tags, front and back. This step will go faster if you stamp a whole bunch of key tags with the same stamp and color before moving to the next stamp and/or color. Let the ink dry.

3 After the front and back of all the key tags have been stamped, arrange them in the order you want them to hang. Use the illustration below to place the tags.

4 Punch small holes in the tags according to the illustration.

5 Take the split rings off the 18 key tags you set aside in step 1. Use these rings to attach the tags in the top row in the illustration.

6 Attach the rings to each other according to the illustration. Hang your curtain with the string or rod.

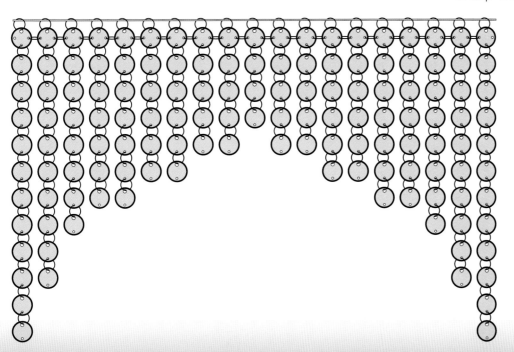

Sticky Foam Stamps

MAKING YOUR OWN STICKY FOAM STAMPS IS SO EASY AND FUN, IT'S HARD TO STOP.

WHAT YOU NEED
→ Sticky-back foam
→ Pencil or pen
→ Scissors or craft knife
→ Jar lid or film canister

WHAT YOU DO

1 Draw your design on the sticky-back foam with the pencil.

2 Cut it out with the scissors. If you need to cut out pieces on the inside of the foam, try using a craft knife.

3 Lay out your sticky-back stamp on the jar lid or film canister. (You can make a stamp on the lid of the film canister or the bottom.) Make sure all the pieces of your stamp will fit.

4 Remove the protective layer covering the adhesive on the back of the sticky-back foam and press it onto the lid.

5 Start stamping!

You can also use foam shapes that are available at craft stores. Some companies sell foam-shaped stickers, so you don't even need glue!

Branching Out Tote Bag

You'll never want to "leaf" this bag home.

WHAT YOU NEED

→ Leaves on branches or just leaves

→ Fabric paint in 4 shades of purple and in silver

→ Canvas tote bag*

→ Scrap cardboard that will fit inside the bag

→ Wax paper

→ Foam paintbrush

→ Brayer

→ Paper towels

→ Iron or use of a clothes dryer

*Available in craft or department stores

WHAT YOU DO

1 Find several bush branches with leaves on them. You can also just use tree leaves. Make sure the branches or leaves have interesting outlines and are fresh and flexible.

2 Lay the tote bag on top of your work space. Slip the piece of scrap cardboard inside the tote bag. This will keep the fabric paint from bleeding through the bag.

3 Figure out where you want the leaves to go on the bag.

4 Squeeze a small amount of the fabric paint you want to use first onto the wax paper.

5 Lay the first branch or leaf facedown on the wax paper. Use the foam paintbrush to coat the underside of the leaf with the paint.

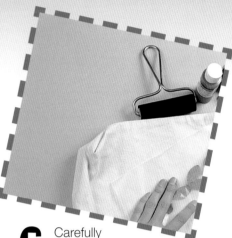

6 Carefully place the painted leaf paint-side down on the bag where you want it. Place a clean sheet of wax paper on top of the branch.

7 Hold the paper and branch still with one hand. Roll the printer's brayer over the branch several times, from many different directions.

8 Carefully peel off the wax paper and the branch. Throw them away. Let the paint dry so that it won't smear when you stamp the next branch or leaf.

9 Repeat steps 4 through 8 with each branch or leaf. Use a different shade of purple each time.

10 Squeeze out a small amount of the silver paint onto another sheet of wax paper. Use the foam paintbrush to put some accents on the leaves. Let the paint dry.

11 Flip the tote bag over and stamp the other side. Either place some paper towels over the prints and have an adult help you iron over them, or place the bag in the dryer on medium heat for 30 minutes to set the ink.

Supersonic Paper Airplanes

Stamped designs will really make your paper airplanes take off.

WHAT YOU NEED

➜ Stamps of your choice

➜ Ink pads in colors of your choice

➜ Card stock

WHAT YOU DO

1 Stamp the piece of card stock with a background image or texture. (We used an old tennis shoe for the plane in the middle.) After the background has dried, stamp different images on top.

2 If you want to accent the fold lines of your airplane with stamps, fold the paper into an airplane and unfold it. Stamp along the creases.

3 Fold your paper airplane, and let it fly!

Velvet Scarf

You don't even need ink to make this elegant scarf, although you will need an adult.

WHAT YOU NEED

→ Butterfly rubber stamp

→ Piece of velvet, at least 18 inches wide and 60 inches long*

→ Spray bottle

→ Iron

→ Fabric pins

→ Sewing needle or sewing machine

→ Thread

*Rayon/acetate velvet works best for this technique. Cotton or silk velvet will work as well, but avoid nylon velvet.

1 Place the stamp with the rubber side facing up on a flat surface. Place the velvet over the stamp so that the back of the velvet is facing you. Make sure the stamp is touching the fabric.

2 Heat the iron to the "high" or "wool" setting. Fill the spray bottle with water and set the nozzle to a "mist" setting.

3 Lightly mist the back of the fabric that's directly over the stamp.

4 Have an adult help you press the iron against the velvet-covered stamp. Count to 15 and see if the stamp has been adequately embossed onto the velvet. (You may need to experiment with timing since different types of velvet require different amounts of time.) If you have a scrap piece of velvet, practice on it first.

5 Repeat this process until you're happy with how the scarf looks.

6 Fold and pin the fabric lengthwise, right sides facing, so that the sides are touching one another and the fabric is in a long, narrow shape.

7 Use a sewing machine or needle and thread to stitch the edge of the pinned fabric. Get an adult to help if you don't know how to sew. Stitch one end of the fabric shut. Turn the velvet "tube" inside out and fold the edges of the open end under. Pin this end and stitch shut.

NOTE: If you want to try this technique but don't want to sew anything, you can emboss stamps on store-bought dresses, shirts, purses, book covers, and more.

Nature Calendar

Find small items such as flowers, rocks, and leaves to decorate this fun project.

WHAT YOU NEED

- → Numbers and alphabet stamp sets
- → Flowers and leaves
- → Black and colored ink pads
- → 12 sheets of 8½ x 11-inch colored card stock
- → Scissors
- → Ruler and pencil
- → 12 sheets of 8½ x 11-inch white card stock
- → Glue stick
- → Scrap paper
- → Heavy books
- → Binder clip
- → Ribbon

WHAT YOU DO

1 Cut each colored card stock page into 35 rectangles approximately 1 x 1½ inches for each month. Use the ruler and pencil to draw grid lines to make the cutting easier.

2 Assign a color for each month, and stamp the dates in the squares. Make sure you create the correct number of days for each month.

3 Draw a straight line about 3 inches from the top of each sheet of white card stock. Stamp the names of the month on each sheet. Let them dry, and erase the pencil marks.

4 Beginning with January, put the days you created in step 1 into columns so that they're in order starting with Sunday and ending with Saturday. Make sure you put the first day on the right day of the week. (Refer to the correct year's calendar.) Use blank squares on days that don't have numbers.

5 Arrange the days until you're happy with where they are, and glue them in place.

6 Cover the calendar page you just completed with a piece of scrap paper and set a heavy book on top of it. Let it dry for at least an hour.

7 When the calendar page has dried, stamp the letter for each day of the week above the column of dates.

8 Decorate the rest of the calendar page by stamping flowers and leaves on it.

9 Repeat steps 4 through 8 for each month of the year.

10 Put all of the calendar pages in order and attach the binder clip to the top. Thread the ribbon through the back binder clip handle and tie a bow to make a hanger for your calendar. Hang it on the wall.

Stamping with Flowers and Leaves

If the flowers and leaves you're working with aren't too big, you can use a regular stamp pad. Lightly press the flower or leaf facedown into the stamp pad. Then press the middle and edges of it onto a piece of paper. Practice on scrap paper until you like how your stamps are turning out. For other ideas on how to stamp with leaves, see page 64.

Glow-in-the-Dark Pillowcase

Rest your head on this heavenly (and comfortable) creation.

WHAT YOU NEED

- Letter and star stamps
- Fabric paints, including glow-in-the-dark paint
- Pillowcase, prewashed and ironed
- Piece of cardboard, about the size of the pillowcase
- Piece of chalk
- Foam paintbrush
- Paper towel
- Iron or use of a clothes dryer

WHAT YOU DO

1 Slide the cardboard inside the pillowcase to prevent the paint from bleeding through onto the other side of the pillowcase.

2 Design the pillowcase and use the chalk to draw out guidelines where you want words and stars to go. This will help you keep your letters even.

3 Brush paint onto the letter stamps. Make sure not to over-ink the stamps. This will allow for crisper letters.

4 Print "Good Night" messages on the pillowcase.

5 Paint the star stamp with glow-in-the-dark paint. Print stars onto the pillowcase.

6 When the pillowcase is finished and the paint is dry, place a paper towel over the stamped areas of the pillow and have an adult help you iron over the pillow. Another way to set the fabric is to throw it in the dryer on medium heat for 30 minutes.

On Your Own

When creating your own designs on fabric, keep these points in mind:

✔ Make sure you've planned out ahead of time what you want to do. Once you stamp onto fabric, you can't wipe it off.

✔ Try not to design anything that looks too busy.

✔ Use different-sized stamps for variety.

✔ Don't use too many colors (no more than six).

Stationery Set

Why buy a stationery set that isn't exactly YOU, when you can make one that perfectly fits your personality?

WHAT YOU NEED

→ Homemade and store-bought stamps

→ Ink pads in colors of your choice

→ Blank stationery

→ Markers

→ Envelopes and cards

→ Sticker paper or blank labels

→ Decorative-edged scissors

WHAT YOU DO

1 Stamp a single image onto the sheets of stationery. If you want, add further decorations with the markers.

2 Make coordinating envelopes and cards by stamping the same image you used on the sheet of stationery. If you want, stamp the image on the envelope or card several times.

3 Stamp one of the stamps onto the sticker paper to make some fake postage. Draw a square or rectangle around it with the markers.

4 Stamp additional images inside the rectangle you just drew. Use letter and number stamps to make them look like fake postage.

5 Cut around the fake postage with the decorative-edged scissors. Peel off the backing and stick them onto the envelope.

Carve a Stamp

THIS STAMP-MAKING PROCESS SHOULD BE DONE ONLY WITH AN ADULT'S HELP: THOSE CUTTERS ARE REALLY SHARP!

WHAT YOU NEED

→ Scrap paper

→ Pencil

→ Tracing paper

→ White vinyl carving material or soft white eraser

→ Linoleum cutter set

→ Straight pin

→ Ink pad

WHAT YOU DO

1 Draw a simple picture on scrap paper. You can use the template on page 108 to make a bird like the one in the project, or you can make something else.

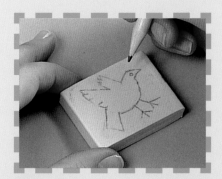

2 Put a piece of tracing paper over your drawing and trace it with the pencil, or just draw it onto the carving material.

3 Put the tracing paper down on the carving material with the pencil marks side down. Lightly scratch over the back of the tracing paper with your fingernail. Lift up a corner of the tracing paper to make sure the pencil marks are transferring to the eraser. Continue scratching at it until the whole design has transferred.

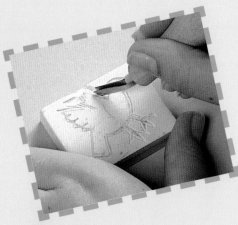

4 With the #1 carving blade (it looks like a small V), carve a shallow line just to the outside of your penciled outline. Make sure to carve away from your hands and body.

5 With the #5 carving blade (it looks like a large U), cut along the outside of the outline you carved in step 4. Make shallow cuts and go slowly.

6 Carve away the rest of the background material with the #5 carving blade.

7 If you'd like to add details to your stamp, use the #1 carving blade. Make thin, shallow lines in the bird's tail to look like feathers. For the bird's eye, poke a pin into the stamp where the eye should go.

8 Ink your stamp and stamp it on a piece of scrap paper. If you'd like to change anything about your stamp, wash the ink off and then carve some more.

Hints for Successful Stamp Carving

✔ Remember, only the raised areas of your stamp will get inked.

✔ If you want words or numbers on your stamp, they have to be reversed in order to come out the right way.

✔ Go slowly when carving your stamp. You can always carve more away, but you can't put it back on once you've taken it off.

With practice, you can make a stamp as intricate as this tree.

All hand-carved stamps on pages 76 and 77 are by Luann Udell.

T-Shirts

Who would have thought you could use a bike
wheel and a boot as stamps!?

Runaway Bike Shirt

AT YOU NEED

→ Mountain bike tire,
  clean and dry

→ Black fabric paint

→ T-shirt

→ Masking tape

→ Paintbrush

→ Large piece of
  scrap fabric
  or cardboard

→ Paper towel

→ Iron or use of a
  clothes dryer

AT YOU DO

1 Find a place suitable for
stamping on the floor, like in
the garage.

2 Lay the T-shirt flat on the
floor, and "measure" how
much of the tire you'll use by
rolling it over the shirt in the
longest direction you want
the tire print. Notice
where the tire
begins to touch
the shirt and
where the
tire rolls
off the
shirt. Mark
those places
off with the
masking tape. This
is the section of the
tire that you'll be con-
cerned with stamping.

Walk-All-Over-Me Shirt

3 Paint the marked-off section of the tire with the black fabric paint. Practice rolling the tire over your scrap fabric or cardboard. You need to apply a lot of your body weight over the tire as you roll it. Practice applying the right amount of pressure on your scrap material before moving onto the clothes you want to stamp.

4 Put a clean piece of cardboard inside the shirt to keep the ink from seeping through to the back of the shirt. Start stamping, remembering to apply as much pressure as you can. Make as many bike trails as you want. Let it dry for several hours, then stamp the back. Follow step 5 of the following instructions to set the ink on the shirt.

WHAT YOU NEED

→ Shoes with interesting soles

→ Black, red, and orange fabric paint

→ T-shirt, washed and dried

→ Piece of cardboard (big enough to fit inside the T-shirt)

→ Foam paintbrush

→ Paper towel

→ Iron or use of a clothes dryer

WHAT YOU DO

1 Put the cardboard inside of the T-shirt.

2 Use the foam brush to paint the fabric paint onto the sole of one of the shoes. Stamp it on the T-shirt.

3 Stamp shoe prints in the different colors all over the front of the shirt.

4 Once the front is dry, turn the shirt over and stamp the back. Let it dry.

5 Place a paper towel over the stamped areas of the T-shirt and have an adult help you iron over it to set the paint. Another way to set the fabric is to throw it in the dryer on medium heat for 30 minutes.

The Cat's Meow

What a purrfect way to decorate an old jean jacket!

WHAT YOU NEED

- → Cat paw stamp or template on page 109
- → Pink fabric paint
- → Denim jacket
- → Wax paper
- → Paper towels
- → Iron or use of a clothes dryer
- → 1 yard fake fur
- → Measuring tape (optional)
- → Scissors
- → Fabric glue

WHAT YOU DO

1 Use the template on page 109 if you want to make your own stamp. Put the denim jacket on your work surface. Squeeze out a small amount of the fabric paint onto the wax paper.

2 Ink the paw print stamp with the fabric paint, and stamp the denim jacket. Start on one side and stamp in different places on it. Let the paint dry, then flip the coat over and stamp the other side.

3 Place a paper towel over the stamped areas of the coat and have an adult help you iron over the fabric paint to set it. Another way to set the fabric is to throw it in the dryer on medium heat for 30 minutes.

4 Figure out where you want the fake fur to go. You can measure those areas with the measuring tape or estimate the length and width of the pieces you need. Cut the pieces out.

5 With the fabric glue, glue the fake fur to the coat. Glue it down in 3- or 4-inch sections. If you have to cover buttons or buttonholes, make a slit in the fake fur where the button or buttonhole is. Then glue down the fake fur, pushing the button through the slit.

Bookmark

Hey, stop folding down the pages in your books. It's easy
to create a bookmark.

WHAT YOU NEED

→ Shoe, purse, and hat rubber stamps

→ Black ink pad

→ White card stock

→ Scissors, ruler, and pencil

→ Purple, magenta, and pink paint

→ Wax paper

→ Foam paintbrush

→ Hole punch

→ Tassel

WHAT YOU DO

1 Cut the card stock to the size you want for the bookmark.

2 Pour a little bit of each color of paint onto the wax paper.

3 Dip the flat end of the foam brush into the paint and use it to decorate the card stock. Let the paint dry before adding a new color.

4 Flip the card stock over and paint the other side.

5 Once the bookmark is dry, stamp the shoe, purse, and hat stamps onto both sides of the card stock.

6 If you want, bring the finished bookmark to a copy center and have it laminated. Then punch a hole in the top and attach the tassel.

The "Turn Off the TV" Stand

Make your television stand more interesting to stare at than your actual television with this creative stamping and collage project.

WHAT YOU NEED

- → Homemade TV stamp
- → Black and pink ink pads
- → TV stand*
- → Pencil and ruler
- → Paper
- → Foam square (size determined in step 2)
- → Masking tape

- → Black acrylic paint
- → Paintbrush
- → Template on page 109
- → Pictures to put in the TVs
- → Scissors
- → White craft glue

*If you don't have a TV stand, you can stamp on any small table or other piece of furniture.

WHAT YOU DO

1 Remove the television from the stand. Throw it away. Paint the stand if you need to.

2 The size of your game board will depend on how big the top of the stand is. Measure the length and width of the top of the stand, and write down your measurements. Subtract a few inches so you have room for captured game pieces. (You'll also have to subtract some more from your length or width if the stand is not square.) Since you'll need eight squares across and eight up and down in order to play checkers or chess, divide your measurements by eight. For example, if the top of your stand measures 16 x 16 inches after you've subtracted a few inches for captured game pieces, divide

by eight to get two. That means each square of your game board will measure 2 x 2 inches.

3 Draw the game board grid with the pencil and ruler. Create a foam stamp that will make stamped squares to fit into the grids you drew. (In the example in step 2, you'd create a 2-inch square stamp.) Stamp squares onto the grid, and let the board dry.

4 To make the black border around the board, use two strips of masking tape to block out a ¼-inch strip around the board. Paint black acrylic paint into the border. Let it dry, and then carefully peel off the masking tape.

5 Use the template on page 109 to carve your own TV stamp. Ink and stamp the TV stamp around the stand wherever you want. Let the ink dry.

6 Cut out cool pictures to put inside the stamped TVs. Glue them to the stamped TVs. If you want the pictures to fit just right, stamp the TV stamp onto a piece of paper. Cut out the TV screen in the stamp. Put it on top of the pictures you want to cut out. Trace around them and cut them out.

Bug Frames

If you're bugging out, stamp a couple of these cool insects and frame yourself.

WHAT YOU NEED

→ Grasshopper and ant rubber stamps

→ Pigment ink pad that can be heat set on glass (same color as frame)

→ Wooden picture frame

→ Dish soap and water

→ Colored paper (that looks nice with the frame)

→ Scissors

→ Photograph that's smaller than the frame

→ Paper towels

→ Use of an oven

WHAT YOU DO

1 Take the glass and backing material out of the frame. Wash the glass with soap and water.

2 Cut a piece of the colored paper so it fits snugly in the frame. Place the backing, paper, photograph, and glass in the frame.

Make sure the photograph is exactly where you want it.

3 Stamp the bugs onto the glass around the photograph. If you don't like the placement of a stamp, wipe it off with a damp paper towel, dry the glass, and try again.

4 Take the glass out of the frame and follow the manufacturer's instructions for setting the ink in the oven. If you want to reverse the stamped images in one frame, simply turn the glass over so the image is facing the back of the frame

Turn Your Artwork into Stamps

ALMOST ANY PRINT SHOP OR OFFICE SUPPLY STORE CAN TAKE YOUR DRAWINGS AND HAVE THEM MADE INTO STAMPS. YOU CAN USE A COPY MACHINE TO REDUCE OR ENLARGE THE IMAGE. TAKE IT TO THE PRINT SHOP AND ASK TO HAVE A RUBBER STAMP MADE OF YOUR DESIGN.

SOME COMPANIES CAN MAKE AN ENTIRE RUBBER SHEET OF YOUR ART. WITH A FEW SIMPLE TOOLS AND SUPPLIES, YOU CAN MOUNT THESE YOURSELF AND MAKE YOUR OWN STAMPS. SEE PAGE 111 FOR MORE INFORMATION.

WHAT YOU NEED

- ➔ Your artwork or clip art
- ➔ Scissors
- ➔ Double-sided self-adhesive foam
- ➔ Pencil
- ➔ Pieces of wood to mount the stamps on
- ➔ Ink pad
- ➔ Scrap paper
- ➔ Glue

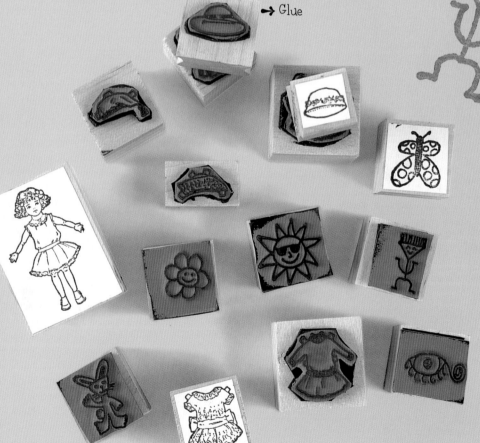

WHAT YOU DO

1 Draw what you want turned into stamps. Make sure the images aren't too detailed or too large. You can also find clip art on your computer or in books. (The paper doll and clothing on this page are from a clip-art book.)

2 Photocopy all of your drawings onto one 8½ x 11-inch piece of paper.

3 Send your drawings away to the company that will turn it into a stamp for you (see page 111). They will send you a sheet of rubber with your images on it.

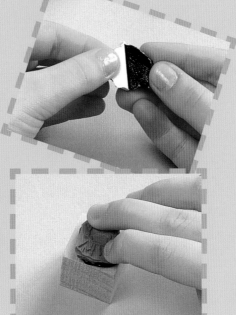

4 After your stamps arrive in the mail, you will have to assemble them. Cut out the first stamp from the sheet of rubber.

5 Put the stamp on double-sided self-adhesive foam and trace around it. Cut out the foam.

6 Peel the protective paper off one side of the double-sided self-adhesive foam. Stick

the rubber stamp onto it. Peel the paper off the other side of the foam and stick it to the block of wood.

7 Ink the stamp and stamp onto a piece of scrap paper. Let the image dry, cut it out, and glue it to the handle of the stamp so you can see what your stamp will look like.

8 Repeat steps 4 through 7 until you have assembled all of your stamps.

The doodle stamps on these pages were created by Doug and Robin Udell.

87

Sun Card

Need a little sunshine in your life? This card will make the Sun pop right out.

WHAT YOU NEED

- ➡ Sun-shaped stamp
- ➡ Black ink pad
- ➡ Dark blue, white, and orange card stock
- ➡ Pencil and ruler
- ➡ Craft chalks or colored pencils
- ➡ Scissors
- ➡ Glue stick
- ➡ Rhinestones with flat backs
- ➡ 1/8-inch hole punch
- ➡ Cutting mat or cardboard
- ➡ Craft knife
- ➡ Bone folder or ball-point pen that's out of ink

WHAT YOU DO

1 Cut a 4 1/4 x 11-inch piece of dark blue card stock. Fold it in half to make the outer card, and set it aside.

2 Cut a 4 1/8 x 10 1/2-inch piece of white card stock. This will be the pop-up part of your card. With the pencil and ruler, lightly draw a line vertically across the middle of the card stock.

3 Ink the rubber stamp with black ink and stamp it in the center of the white card stock.

4 Stamp the image again on another piece of white card stock.

5 Color the suns with the chalks or colored pencils. See page 18 for more information on working with chalks and colored pencils. Cut out the second sun you stamped. This sun is for the front of the card.

6 Glue small rhinestones to the design and use a small hole punch. Don't cut, punch, or add rhinestones to that middle line you drew in step 2.

7 Place the sun design on the cutting mat or cardboard. Use the craft knife to cut along the top and bottom of the whole image (including any other decorations you drew). Don't cut on the left or right side of the image.

Sun Card

8 If you want, make additional decorative cuts in and around the stamp. For example, you can cut out paper inside the Sun's rays.

9 Put the ruler on the pencil line you drew in step 2. Use the bone folder or ballpoint pen to score along the pencil line

above and below the stamped image. Reposition the ruler along the left edge of the image and score it again. Do the same on the right side of the image.

10 Fold the card stock along the scored line in the center, carefully pulling the stamped image toward you as

you fold. The creases above and below the image make a "valley" or V fold. The stamped image itself will have a "mountain" fold, while the score lines along either side will become "valleys." Once the card stock is folded correctly, rub the bone folder along the outside of the card stock to crease the folds.

11 Glue the pop-up to the inside of the dark blue outer card. Erase the pencil line.

12 Glue the sun that you colored and cut out earlier to the front of the card with a strip of orange card stock (see photo on page 89 for placement).

Polystyrene Foam

POLY WHAT? POLYSTYRENE FOAM, YOU KNOW, THE STUFF USED TO MAKE TAKE-OUT FOOD BOXES, COFFEE CUPS, AND PACKING TRAYS FOR MEAT. THIS STUFF IS PERFECT FOR STAMPING. USE AN ENTIRE TRAY AS A PRINTING BLOCK, OR CUT A CONTAINER INTO SMALLER PIECES TO USE AS STAMPS.

WHAT YOU NEED

➜ Polystyrene foam tray (for a printing block)

➜ Marker

➜ Pencil or ballpoint pen

➜ Ink pad

➜ Paper

➜ Brayer

WHAT YOU DO

1 Clean the tray with hot soapy water and dry it with a towel.

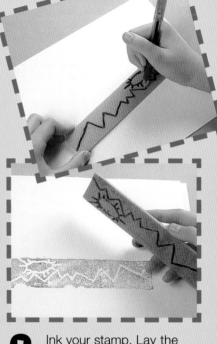

2 To make a printing block, set a piece of the tray upside down on a table. Draw your design on the tray with a marker, and then use a pencil or ballpoint pen to carve the image into the tray. The design can be as simple or complicated as you like. Note: If there's a raised imprint or code on the tray, it'll show up in the design.

3 Ink your stamp. Lay the stamp on a piece of scrap paper. Roll the brayer over the stamp, or rub it with your hand to transfer the design. Slowly peel back a corner of the stamp to see if the printing worked. If it looks good, then go ahead and peel the rest of the stamp off. If the design isn't clear, press the corner of it back down and roll the brayer over it a few more times before lifting it again.

To make individual stamps, use a craft knife to cut designs from a piece of polystyrene, then glue cardboard, bottle caps, lids, or film canisters to the backs of the designs.

Celestial Charm Bracelet

Create spacey charms for this bracelet and watch them shrink before your eyes.

WHAT YOU NEED

→ Stamps of aliens, spaceships, and stars

→ Blue, purple, and fuchsia pigment or fabric ink pads (or colors that match the beads you're using)

→ Round object about 2 inches in diameter (such as a flashlight or food container lid)

→ Clear shrink plastic

→ Permanent marker

→ Scissors

→ Hole punch

→ Templates on page 109 (optional)

→ Nonstick cookie sheet

→ Use of an oven

→ Jump rings

→ Two pairs of round-nosed pliers

→ Memory wire bracelet (about 2½ loops)

→ Mix of different-sized beads

1 Put the round object on top of the shrink plastic. Trace around it with the permanent marker. Make seven circles and cut them out with the scissors.

2 Punch a hole in the top of each plastic circle with the hole punch. Leave at least ⅛ inch of plastic between the edge of the circle and the hole.

3 If you're making your own stamps, use the templates on page 109 if you want.

4 Stamp the images onto the plastic circles. Vary the colors of ink you use.

5 Put the stamped circles on the nonstick cookie sheet and follow the manufacturer's instructions for baking the shrink plastic.

6 To open the first jump ring, put the nose of each pair of pliers on either side of the opening in the jump ring. Bend one end of the ring toward you and the other away. Place one of the plastic circles on the jump ring. Close it by bending the ends together again. Put a jump ring on each piece of shrink plastic.

Celestial Charm Bracelet

7 Wrap one end of the memory wire around the nose of the pliers. Make a little loop to hold the beads in place.

8 String the beads and charms onto the bracelet. When you're finished, bend the other end of the memory wire with the pliers, as you did in step 7.

Sock It to 'Em

Turn a pair of simple white socks into a colorful fashion statement.

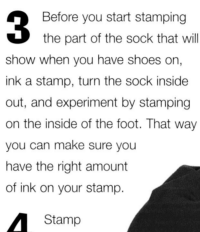

WHAT YOU NEED

→ Heart-shaped stamps

→ Red or pink fabric ink pad

→ Pair of socks (don't use tube socks or heavy sweat socks)

→ Pencil

→ Thin cardboard

→ Scissors

→ Paper towels

→ Iron or use of a clothes dryer

WHAT YOU DO

1 Trace one of the socks onto the piece of cardboard. Cut it out.

2 Slip the piece of cardboard you just cut out into the first sock. This will keep the ink from bleeding through to the other side when you stamp.

3 Before you start stamping the part of the sock that will show when you have shoes on, ink a stamp, turn the sock inside out, and experiment by stamping on the inside of the foot. That way you can make sure you have the right amount of ink on your stamp.

4 Stamp your first sock. After the ink has dried, turn the sock over and stamp the other side. Remove the cardboard and stamp the other sock.

5 Either place some paper towels over the socks and have an adult help you iron over them, or place the socks in the dryer on medium heat for 30 minutes.

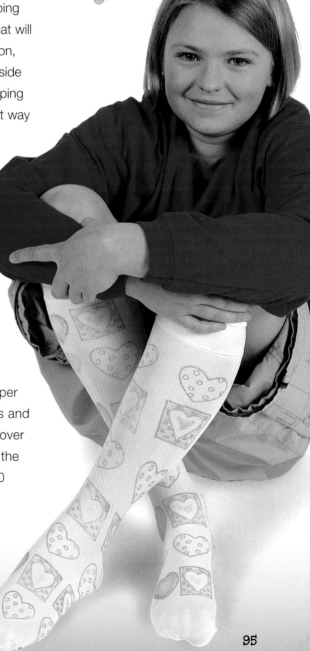

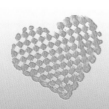

Fossil Bookplate

Make no bones about it; this project is positively prehistoric.

WHAT YOU NEED

→ Fossil stamp
  (see page 97)

→ Brown and black
  ink pads

→ Beige, tan, and brown
  acrylic paints

→ Wax paper

→ Foam paintbrush

→ Large self-adhesive
  label

WHAT YOU DO

1 Put a small amount of each color of acrylic paint onto the wax paper. With the foam paintbrush, paint the background of the blank label light beige. Let it dry, and then lightly apply the other acrylic paints onto the label to finish the background.

Toothpick Stamps

You can also use pieces of string, thin straws, or anything else you can come up with.

WHAT YOU NEED

→ Toothpicks

→ Old mouse pad or thick craft foam

→ Scissors

→ Craft glue

WHAT YOU DO

1 Create a stamp design. If you're interested in creating the fossil stamp use the template on page 108.

2 Lay out the toothpicks on the foam in the design you've chosen for the stamp.

3 Cut the toothpicks to fit with the scissors, and glue them in place with the craft glue.

2 Ink the fossil stamp with the brown ink pad. Stamp it onto the label and let it dry.

3 Ink the fossil stamp with the black ink pad. Stamp it over the brown fossil image. Don't worry about lining up the stamp exactly with the first image—it'll look much cooler if you don't.

4 Paint a rectangle above the fossil. (You can also create a toothpick stamp in the shape of a rectangle.)

5 Use the side of the foam paintbrush to make a triangle border around the label.

Funky Daisy Curtains

Liven up a plain set of curtains with this stamping technique.

WHAT YOU NEED

→ Flower stamps

→ New pencils with erasers

→ Acrylic fabric paints

→ Fabric paint pens

→ Plastic sheeting or old newspaper

→ Plain cotton or poly-ester curtains, washed and dried

→ Foam paintbrush

→ Iron or use of a clothes dryer

WHAT YOU DO

1 Spread the plastic sheeting or old newspaper over your work space. Put the first curtain on top.

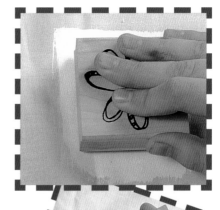

2 Using the foam paintbrush, paint white rectangles on the curtains. Position the rectangles randomly or make a pattern out of them if you want. Let them dry.

3 Ink the flower stamp. Stamp it on top of the white rectangles and in between them.

98

4 Once the paint dries, stamp dots around the borders of the rectangle with the pencil erasers. If you want, add a smaller dot on top of each of the larger dots. Wait until the first dots dry before adding the second ones.

5 After the flower stamps have dried, use the fabric paint pens to add color if you want.

6 When the curtain is finished and the paint is dry, place a paper towel over the stamped areas of the curtain and have an adult help you iron over them. Another way to set the fabric is to throw it in the dryer on medium heat for 30 minutes.

Frog Umbrella

Make a splash jumping over puddles like a you-know-what
with this festive umbrella.

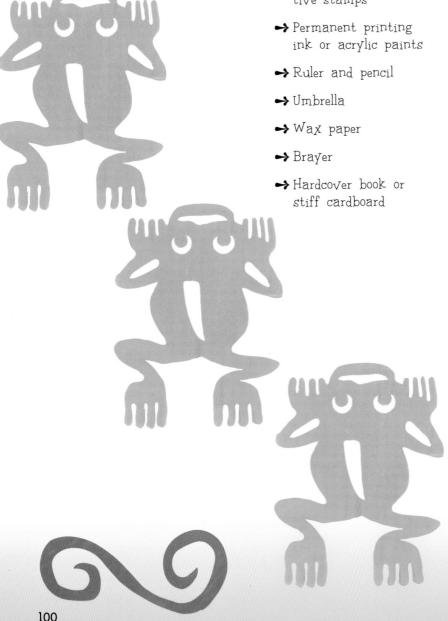

WHAT YOU NEED

→ Foam frog and decorative stamps

→ Permanent printing ink or acrylic paints

→ Ruler and pencil

→ Umbrella

→ Wax paper

→ Brayer

→ Hardcover book or stiff cardboard

WHAT YOU DO

1 If you'd like to plan the placement of the stamps, use the ruler and pencil to find the center of each section of the opened umbrella. Mark them lightly with the pencil.

2 Put a small amount of the ink on the wax paper. Roll over it with the brayer until you've coated the brayer with a thin layer of ink.

3 Hold the frog stamp in one hand and roll the brayer over it from side to side and up and down. Make sure the stamp is coated with a thin, even layer of ink.

4 Place the book underneath the section of the umbrella you're about to stamp. This will give you a hard surface to press the stamp onto. (This is also a good place to recruit an extra pair of hands to help you.)

5 Stamp the frog stamp onto the umbrella. Hold the fabric with one hand while you pull the stamp off.

6 Ink the decorative stamp the same way you inked the frog. Stamp it on either side of the frog stamp.

7 Stamp all the sections of the umbrella in this way.

8 Put the umbrella in a safe place to dry. Make sure it dries for at least 24 hours before you fold or use it.

Bug Box

Stamped bugs sure are cute, even if you can't stand the real ones. And you can always use the box for something else.

WHAT YOU NEED

→ Flower and ladybug stamps

→ Ink pads in colors of your choice

→ Acrylic paint and paintbrush (optional)

→ Wooden bug box

→ Ribbon

→ Drill (optional)

WHAT YOU DO

1 Paint the wooden box if you want.

2 Stamp the flower along the bottom edge of the box.

3 Stamp the ladybug randomly around the box. When stamping around corners, press the stamp onto one side of the box. Put your fingers on top of the stamp where it overlaps with the corner, and then slowly press it onto the other side.

4 Thread the ribbon through holes on either side of the box, and tie a knot in both ends on the inside to make a handle. If your box has no holes, either have an adult help you drill some, or skip the ribbon.

Add Pizzazz to Your Scrapbooks

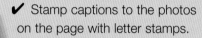

WITH LITTLE MORE THAN A FEW STAMPS AND SOME INK PADS YOU CAN TURN ANY SCRAP-BOOK OR PHOTO ALBUM INTO A FUN-FILLED MEMORY BOOK.

Here are some tips for decorating your pages with stamps:

✔ Stamp captions to the photos on the page with letter stamps.

✔ Remember when things happened by stamping the dates onto the pages.

✔ Record your thoughts and feelings by writing about them with letter stamps or carving stamps that reflect your feelings.

✔ Use stamps to make frames around the pictures.

✔ Stamp backgrounds to the pages with found objects that have cool textures.

✔ Stamp on the pages with a piece of sponge to create cool backgrounds. You can use a regular sponge for this or the special sponges sold at craft stores.

✔ Glue or stamp leaves and flowers on your pages.

✔ Make peek-through windows by cutting a hole in the page in front of where you will put the photo or stamp. Then position whatever you want to have peeking through the window on the next page and glue it into place.

Aqua Board

Unlike real fish, you'll never have to feed these little critters.

WHAT YOU NEED

→ Seahorse and fish stamps

→ Acrylic paint in colors of your choice

→ Wooden framed bulletin board

→ Turquoise semigloss paint

→ Foam paintbrush

→ Turquoise, dark green, pale green, orange, and blue craft foam

→ Scissors

→ Craft glue

→ Wax paper

→ White paint

→ Paintbrush

→ Permanent marker

WHAT YOU DO

1 Paint the wooden frame of the bulletin board with the turquoise semigloss paint. Let it dry.

2 Cut seaweed shapes out of the turquoise, dark green, and pale green craft foam. Glue them onto the bulletin board.

3 Stamp the seahorse stamp onto the orange craft foam. Let it dry, and then cut it out and glue it to the bulletin board.

4 Squeeze a small amount of each color of acrylic paint onto the wax paper. With the foam brush, dab different colors onto the first fish stamp.

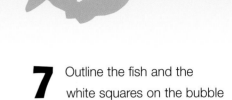

Stamp it onto the bulletin board. Repeat until you've stamped all the fish you want.

6 Paint a white square onto each bubble so they look three dimensional. Let the paint dry.

7 Outline the fish and the white squares on the bubble with a permanent marker.

5 Cut circles out of the blue craft foam for bubbles. Glue them onto the bulletin board.

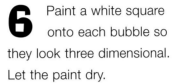

Key Chain

Keep track of your keys using these stamped ID tags.

WHAT YOU NEED

→ Small stamp of your choice

→ Black ink

→ Metal ID tag

→ Copper embossing powder and heat gun

WHAT YOU DO

1 See page 45 for more information on heat embossing. Ink the stamp and stamp it onto the metal circle.

2 Quickly pour the embossing powder over the stamp. Make sure you do this while the ink's still wet.

3 Tap the excess embossing powder off the tag.

4 Preheat the heat gun for about 10 seconds. Hold it 4 inches above the ID tag to melt the embossing powder. You'll see the powder melt, rise up, and get shiny. Turn off the heat gun.

5 Wait for the metal to cool completely before touching it.

106

Window Ornaments

These look great just about anywhere.

WHAT YOU NEED

→ Large stamps

→ Black ink pad

→ Card stock

→ Clear embossing powder and heat gun (optional)

→ Markers or colored pencils

→ Scissors

→ Glue

→ Hole punch

→ Ribbon, string, or wire

WHAT YOU DO

1 Ink the first stamp and stamp it onto a piece of card stock.

2 Emboss the image if you want (see page 45).

3 Make another image on a different piece of card stock and emboss it if you want.

4 Color in both images with the markers.

5 Cut around the images carefully, leaving some of the card stock around the edges of the image. Glue them back to back.

6 Punch a hole (or holes) in the top of the ornament with the hole punch. Thread the ribbon, string, or wire through the hole and hang it.

Templates

When working with templates, you can do one of the following:

→ Tape a piece of tracing paper over the template in the book. Trace all the lines marked on the template. Untape the template and cut it out.

→ Lay a piece of tracing paper on the back of the paper you're using for your project. Make sure the chalky side of the tracing paper is facing down. Lay a copy of the template on top of the tracing paper, and trace the shape with a sharp pencil. The image will appear on the project paper.

→ Take this book to a copy center. Photocopy and enlarge the template you want to use until it's the right size. Cut off the excess paper.

→ Scan the template with a computer scanner, enlarge it if you need to, and print.

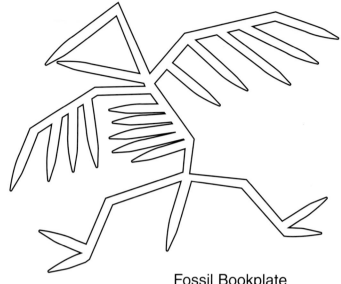

Fossil Bookplate
page 96

Stationery Set
page 76

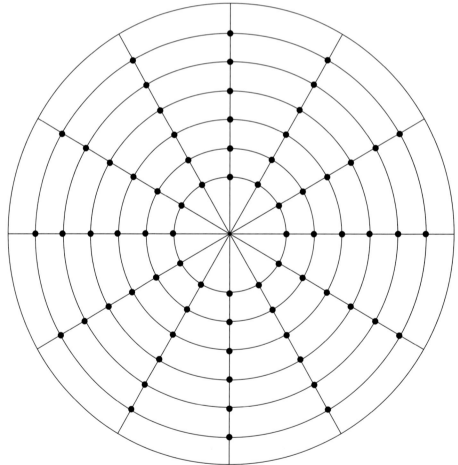

Hypnotic CD Clock
page 36

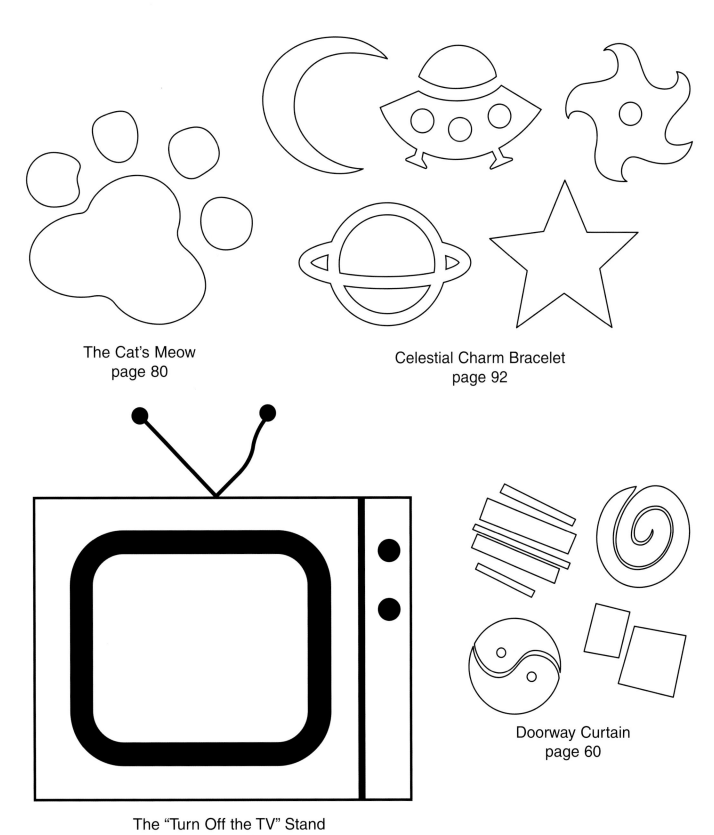

The Cat's Meow
page 80

Celestial Charm Bracelet
page 92

The "Turn Off the TV" Stand
page 82

Doorway Curtain
page 60

Stamp Information

The Stamps Used In This Book

If you'd like to use the exact same stamps that we used in some of our projects, here's where they came from:

Starlight Gift Wrap
Personal Stamp Exchange
Giant Duffel Bag
Chunky Foam Stamps
Simply Divine Sneakers
Diffusion
Dog Bowl and Plate
Bone, Dog and Fire Hydrant: Plaid
Enterprises
Fork, Spoon, and Knife: Hot Potatoes
Flower Power Cards
Chunky Stamps
Sun Card
Anita's Art Stamps, Sugarloaf Products
Supersonic Paper Airplanes
Chunky Stamps
Garden Party
Hero Arts
Sock It To 'Em!
Dotted Heart: **Creative Beginnings**
Checkered Heart & Reverse Heart:
Inkadinkado
Bountiful Heart: **Rubber Stampede**
Sunflower Lampshade
Chunky Stamps
Paper Bag Bookcover
Chunky Stamps
Nature Calendar
Hero Arts
Aqua Board
Chunky Stamps
Velvet Scarf
Inkadinkado
Glow-in-the-Dark Pillowcase
Stars: **Chunky Stamps**
Letters: **Plaid Enterprises**
Bookmark
Personal Stamp Exchange
Window Ornaments
Butterfly: **Inkadinkado**
Tribal: **Personal Stamp Exchange**
Funky Daisy Curtains
Heartfelt Impressions
Frog Umbrella
Chunky Stamps
Bug Frames
All Night Media, Plaid Enterprises
Bug Box
Rubber Stampede

Some of these companies will sell their stamps to you on-line or through the mail. Others will help you find a retail store in your area that carries their stamps.

Chunky Foam Stamps
Duncan Enterprises
www.duncancrafts.com
5673 E. Shields Ave
Fresno, CA 93727
Tel: 1-800-438-6226
Fax: (559) 291-9444

Creative Beginnings
www.creativebeginnings.com

Diffusion
www.hamptonart.com

Heartfelt Impressions
www.heartfeltimpressions.com

Hero Arts
www.heroarts.com
1343 Powell Street
Emeryville, CA 94608
Tel: 1-800-822-4376
Fax: 1-800-441-3632
All Hero Arts designs and products are original and copyrighted. The purchaser of a Hero Arts product is granted a limited license to use such product, for personal, noncommercial use only. Reproduction of Hero Arts products or images in any way for either commercial use or in an inappropriate manner is prohibited without written consent. Hero Arts is an Angel company and will grant, with a written request, commercial use for up to 50 handstamped images. See http://www.heroart.com for complete details.

Hot Potatoes
www.hotpotatoes.com
2805 Columbine Place
Nashville, TN 37204
Tel: (615) 269-8002
Fax: (615) 269-8004

Inkadinkado
www.inkadinkado.com
61 Holton St
Woburn, MA 01801
Tel: 1-800-888-4652
Fax: 1-800-329-4657

Personal Stamp Exchange
www.psxdesign.com
Tel: 1-800-782-6748
Fax: (707) 588-7476

All Night Media
Plaid Enterprises, Inc.
Norcross, GA
www.plaidonline.com
Tel: 1-800-842-4197

Rubber Stampede, Inc.
www.rubberstampede.com
2550 Pellissier Place
Whittier, CA 90601
Tel: (562) 695-7969
Fax: (562) 695-4227

Sugarloaf Products
www.sugarloafproducts.com

Acknowledgments

The projects in this book were created by these big kids at heart:

Irene Dean is the author of the awesome Lark book, *Kids' Crafts: Polymer Clay*. Her project is the Polymer Clay Notepad Cover on page 57.

Dietra Garden is an art educator and freelance designer. Her projects are the Flower Power Cards on page 42, Frog Umbrella on page 100, Window Ornaments on page 107, Bug Box on page 102, Sock It to 'Em on page 95, Add Pizzazz to Your Scrapbooks on page 103, and the Key Chain on page 106.

Lynn Krucke is a mixed-media artist in Summerville, SC whose interests include paper arts, beads, fiber, fabric, and polymer clay. Lynn's project is the Sun Card on page 88.

Marthe Le Van has been a curator, exhibition manager, and a craft designer. She is currently an editor for Lark Books. Her Sunny Citrus Picture Frame appears on page 26.

Diana Light is a D. Light-ful (get it!) artist who has this uncanny ability to make everything she touches look absolutely fabulous and instantly cool. Her projects are the Hypnotic CD Clock on page 36, Branching Out Tote Bag on page 64, The "Turn Off the TV" Stand on page 82, Bug Frames on page 84, and Celestial Charm Bracelet on page 92.

Joan Morris is a general designer and business owner who has created many designs for Lark Books. She works and lives in Asheville, N.C. Her projects are the Giant Duffel Bag on page 24, Dog Bowl and Mat on page 34, Too Cool Bandannas on page 40, Sunflower Lampshade on page 48, Paper Bag Book Cover on page 50, Boot T-Shirt on page 78, Fossil Bookplate on page 96, Bookmark on page 81, and Aqua Board on page 104.

Timothy Saunders is a yoga teacher, costume designer, and all around creative genius. His projects are the Bike Tire T-Shirt on page 78 and The Cat's Meow on page 80.

Kathryn Temple is a nationally recognized visual artist based in Asheville, NC. Her projects are the Hand Towel on page 30, Velvet Scarf on page 68, and Glow-in-the-Dark Pillowcase on page 72.

Terry Taylor is such a wonderful guy that we don't have enough room here to expound on his many fine attributes. His projects are the Simply Divine Sneakers on page 32, Big Birthday Platter on page 46, and Funky Daisy Curtains on page 98.

Karen Timm is a paper, fiber, and book artist who lives in Madison, WI. Her projects are Doorway Curtain on page 60 and Supersonic Paper Airplanes on page 66.

Luann Udell is an award-winning, nationally exhibited mixed-media artist who lives in Keene, NH. She is the author of *Carving Rubber Stamps*, published by Lark Books. Her projects are the Stationery Set on page 74 and Turn Your Artwork into Stamps on page 86.

Amy Van Aarle is an artist and designer who lives in a little seaside town in Massachusetts. Her passion is her greeting card company, *little paper company*, where she designs her cards from cut paper (www.littlepapercompany.com). Her projects are the Starlight Gift Wrap on page 22, Garden Party on page 52, and Nature Calendar on page 70.

More Much Needed Thank Yous:

The wonderful crew of kids who posed for pictures, tested and made projects, and gave us their all: **Jasmine Sky Figlow, Summer Griffin, Shirah Lee, Corrina Matthews, Isaac Paul, Natasha Perez, Niroshka Perez, JJ Peterson, Jazzman Peterson, Ray Ray Peterson, Moriah Sky Rullmoss, Kayla Wolhart,** and **Dylan Wolhart**

And, **Terry Taylor, Katherine Aimone, Marthe Le Van** (for pitching in), **Kathy Holmes** (for her creative design and relaxed attitude), **Evan Bracken** (for his wonderful photography), **Shannon Yokeley, Jodi Ford, Dina Paul, Beverly Peterson, Cindy Zalman-Wolhart, Ellie Lee, Nancy Griffin, Todd Schupp, Grace Harrison, Denisa Rullmoss,** and **Art Snyder.**

Final thanks to **Luann, Robin,** and **Doug Udell**—mad stampers, all.

A Note About Suppliers

Usually, the supplies you need for making the projects in Lark books can be found at your local craft supply store, discount mart, home improvement center, or retail shop relevant to the topic of the book. Occasionally, however, you may need to buy materials or tools from specialty suppliers. In order to provide you with the most up-to-date information, we have created a listing of suppliers on our Website, which we update on a regular basis. Visit us at www.larkbooks.com, click on "Craft Supply Sources," and then click on the relevant topic. You will find numerous companies listed with their web address and/or mailing address and phone number.

Metric Conversion Chart

$\frac{1}{16}$ inch = 2 mm
$\frac{1}{8}$ inch = 3 mm
$\frac{1}{4}$ inch = 6 mm
$\frac{1}{2}$ inch = 1.3 cm
$\frac{3}{4}$ inch = 1.9 cm
1 inch = 2.5 cm
$1\frac{1}{2}$ inches = 3.8 cm
2 inches = 5.1 cm
$2\frac{1}{2}$ inches = 6.4 cm
3 inches = 7.6 cm
$3\frac{1}{2}$ inches = 8.9 cm
4 inches = 10.2 cm
$4\frac{1}{2}$ inches = 11.4 cm
5 inches = 12.7 cm
6 inches =15.2 cm
7 inches = 17.8 cm
8 inches = 20.3 cm
9 inches = 22.9 cm
10 inches = 25.4 cm

To convert inches to centimeters, multiply by 2.5.

To convert ounces to grams, multiply by 28.

To convert fluid ounces to milliliters, multiply by 30.

To convert yards to meters, multiply by .9.

Index